SPITSHINE

SPITSHINE

ANNE MARIE ROONEY

CARNEGIE MELLON UNIVERSITY PRESS

PITTSBURGH 2012

ACKNOWLEDGMENTS

Thanks to the following journals, in which many of the poems in this collection first appeared: *Abjective, Bat City Review, Bateau, Bellevue Literary Review, Coconut, Columbia, Crazyhorse, Gulf Coast, The Iowa Review, La Fovea, Leveler, LIT, Narrative, Ninth Letter, Octopus, Parthenon West Review, Pleiades, Subtropics, Typo,* and *Vinyl.*

"Sabbath for a Dry Season" was reprinted in the *Best New Poets 2008* anthology. "What my heart is turning" was reprinted in the *Best American Poetry 2011* anthology.

Thank you to Ken McClane and Alice Fulton for their wisdom, guidance, inspiration, example; to Michael Koch and Helena Viramontes for seeing me through it; to David L. Picket, for his generous support as this manuscript took shape; and to the Cornell workshop and community, for time and space and eyes and ears.

Thanks to the Pittsburgh School, the Friendship Cohort, et al. Thanks to the New York people, the village kids, et cetera. Thanks to Kip Zegers, Lori D'Amico, Jim Daniels, and Jerry Costanzo. Thanks to Lillian-Yvonne Bertram, Ezra D. Feldman, Ben Pelhan, and Julia Rooney.

Finally, to Tom, my heart.

Book design: Veronica Kawka

Library of Congress Control Number 2011926208
ISBN 978-0-88748-550-3

10 9 8 7 6 5 4 3 2 1

CONTENTS

This book is for

Erica Melack Rooney and Peter Rooney,

my parents.

1

DOMESTIC

There is a house to me. When Saturday leaves a gradient

of onion on the floor I open a mouth which is also a corner.

Who can say this also isn't mine? The sparrow of belong-to

has smaller than nowhere to fit. If I could feed the trellis in daisies

I would not. I would not feed the trellis or that which has never sweat

against a screen door or door. (Which can't be mine

either.) (Each plank fretted up as if mistakenly gardened.)

I would never water the ankles of anything. I think we should begin

at the head, the think-prickle: If I could be paid in water earned back

I would crater the kitchen and stop the smokestack.

Instructions for wooing me (monster that I am)

First generate a charge. Rub hard if you have to. Crash a little against
my fleeciest spots. When I begin to stain with electricity, turn your faucets
off. I am a pornography of small promises. I tell you this softly because really
I am a soft thing. I open my modesty umbrella. This is how you know to get out
your cutting board. If I balk pull a tooth or two. I want you to do this to me
because I want you to do this. I am the chugging gin of the universe. I balm
and bomb. In your mind I burn like thirty watts of unstrained honey.
I am not very bright with my antennae on. With diamonds
and things that are less than diamonds on. Like a lone languid
heat storm, you say. I say The ribcage is not a sensible machinery.
But I am dimmer even than the face of a leap year. Stop me if I start
to speak of terror. It is a habit unbecoming of being here. It is not good
for your sauna perspective. Is my surge protector paling? I pale
to speak of it. In the jar rimmed with pollen is a knife with your name on it.
Have I told you about the big development? You are dreaming
of me now. If I am glowing like a firefly know that I am not
a firefly. This time of night every bee dusts with a little sparkling blow. Blow me
back to the square I came from. It's your move, I say. You move an inch
away. Step seven: I turn red as a city. Step eight: I become a little less
uniform. I sprout seven more whiskers. I hiss like a fire house
expelling its heroes. You know what to do. I can tell by your glasses.
If map then midriff. If shot glass then novocaine. That will be all
my surnames on the floor. I'm fair game, Joe. It's always open season
on princesses.

Flower Sonnet

The way bravery tails out sharply like
the staunch come-on, creature of more wanting
even than me. When we met, my wanting
him was tangential to the pinch. It's like
my mother said before she slumped in: like
it or like its petals. Even wanting
turns over. The way I opened, wanting
more even than him. And so I was like
the stinger already having scooped whole
pits. How does need, and can it really be
crossed under? This well from which oh my whole
me-ness shakes down. If hot is what he'll be
I'll spread a honey too. Two can play bee
to that pluck. Even smarting is a hole.

LIFE ON THE MEAN

Because my hair was black, I never washed it. When the butcher asked
for his penny I gave him one wink and a hard dime. I was in debt
to no one, not the men with crumpled faces who sat on the corner
drinking coffee till dawn, not January's homeless firs. I wrapped my garbage
in saris and left it to spoil in the sun. Alley cats slunk back to their alleys
when they saw me coming. Spiders gathered on my crooked sill
in fear. The neighbors prayed, for I was quiet as strychnine. I wore nothing
but silver and when the rain came shone like an angry planet. I had no orbit,
just pitchers and pitchers of tonic water. In the evening I played blackjack
with my cockatoo. I swallowed steak without chewing or homely remorse.
This was the last year I owned a purse.

GRUDGE PASTORAL

Edge 1

My feelings are hard as a beautiful
kidney. They jiggle
the rivets. They make a romp of
this busty throng, this lacuna
of sense, this me stealing away
in the winking angle of your wale.

Edge 2

Because underneath my pants I am wearing
stockings and underneath those a sappy lacy
thing and underneath those just my skin evening
out for one last round on the house.
Because you take all of these off and stare
at the rabid gaga I hold out for you.
Because it is woozy, how I hold myself
out, how abashed, how I pretend
I have pockets and then check them

twice (the trick here prone
as the depth of your hand).

Edge 3

You deadbolt. I chastity
belt. You buckling
anchor. I torch another.
You start in your sleep.
Time pinches back to the marring
moment: I : crush : you.

Edge 4

How abashed should a predator
be? I predate her. If this ditz stint
is through, I will make a feral
fuckery of you.

Dirty Story

2.

I look out from my spire of fuss and buzzkill. A carriage is awaking on the hill.
The sun shifts and maybe it is you come for the annual tap. Last year you rode right up
and with your spurs aglitter clicked your tongue. Did you think I was a home? I would
buckle under you? I look again and the angle of everything has changed. There is no sun
here and I am the sun, that starched, appalled. The something I have become
is truly unbecoming.

5.

Your wink sugars down my spine. I think: I want to take a bath. I think: Am I a red bulb
or am I something lower. For hours I do nothing
but talk to the squall. The many whistles of bird through water become one
dull hum, which I stop hearing two cloudbreaks in. Though
the room is dark I shutter it, sit in the dark, am dark with a dark
hole. I should never call myself
a hole.

3.

On the third day I feel a start in my middle scar—there is no word but the word
for anger, the revolting dog lapping rough and everywhere. If I am this sharp
I would rather not be. I preen the feathers of your tribute, and they sag forward. Dulled
luster, I would rather be prone than hard-won.

4.

All I got's this window, this turning red. Through the night, it holds itself between me
and blacker. It saves my hide. It keeps me hidden. In this it is like a skin, but it is not your
skin, your sweet and cold and blue. The things I would do if I had you for a shoe.

1.

The hero thought me wicked
His mother made me moan
I shot shotguns
I rode shotgun
I never went home

DOMESTIC

From my kernel to the nubby top is a tipping
matter, a how much April can he fit into
his hourly already-came. How passing
becomes past & into, then, a hundred thumbs,
into like ink or a face: how I am unable to stay, in
my rounding head, anyone's kick-cat. This is the one
that sounds dropped. That the boy
loved me & loved seeing me asides itself. I assuaged
all the eyes in him. And this one
sound, always of bone-knockers, place to which stairs travel,
but never return, sound always of sex in the attic, place of stairs
that stop upwards. I have had thoughts. I have also been thinking
of you.

HASP PASTORAL

Edge 1

I am annually arranged.
You solder my wrists to the morning's slow hinge.
I come to be more than just a goosy tether.
You take and you take me to an undercover place.
I wipe out beneath the woven rim.
You delight in the purple fixture of me.

I turn another color. ## Edge 2

My trick punch. My bum smile. My soddered
and still-sticky. My indexed perennials. My pedals
need oil. My mischief in the kitchen. My android
of desire. My vaulted breast-stuff. My bedtime
lure. My throe in the wrong. My throw me a bone.
My fastening. My suture. My crooks bluff-high.

Edge 3

In the ever-demoning
lap of midnight, you start
to elaborate: I am coming
unsewn—thoughtlessly—a show pigeon
of screwy measures. All the answers
to this hitching are in the fret of the thing,
but I hem and haw, sleight-caught.

You abet and abet, even when love
is the subject.

Edge 4

This is the end of my appeal.

When I make a hook of myself
the sky turns the yellow
of three-day bruises. I give you the whole
snare of me.

2

Face Sonnet

My face is hard-like, cold, or the crack one,
I mean I, ply open. It caves into
a blackening screen which scares the light. To
say this marriage works itself lessens: one
way is a kitchen in moonshine; one
draws its own wet. My face is to
you as the cut is to clean. But these two
things do sync. So is treachery. The one
time night bloated me out of my crisp, you
came up like a flame-soaked sheet. My face
had never quickened in storm, and craved you
for your wider dry. If you knew my face
you didn't say but shone your bluest phase,
its shadow cleaved anew. So I earned you.

I DID A SERIES IN A VERY HOT AUGUST

Of men able and disabled
about me, a memory

to make stone in:

The wave and wilder

Shores of love

At which the mark meant
I am my self

*The white phrase in 20 minutes
of tearing*

Cloth

*The waiting
shows*

Traces blowing their tracings

*That nothing that lies
behind*

One over-written

*The beginning, in which he
uses the sustain
and I dance all around*

*He who comes upon another
becoming*

*My works the encounter
into which he puts his name*

This window is not this window

*In the dark all sorts of things are
put in me*

In that complex scandal

*Possibly always
drawing the prosthesis*

Or if you like difference

*Its hard ache was me who was
an outsider*

Ignore me so

Blind-become

*The friendship of war
which never turns
or touches*

Of impossible light

Up on each other one

Me

Again

Beautifully

Something

and

There is continuous war

ABOUT THE NECK

What is it about the neck. (The charge).

(Discharge). What's about the neck (if

air stops). And come throttle in me a gasp-large

scoop. The choke is set like nothing

else: like under steam is a whistle. Is it

the steam that moves I mean. If the air

stops from its fall, break. The neck is

an urn then. (A Pipe. Gully. Monster.)

This has no end, no – I don't think – stopper.

A tunnel withouts every question. So will show

my passage its own passage out. Or, I was a knife

with that white straw not knowing. What is that.

And does a hole remember its shovel. (Depression).

The air around it mars it. Light *prints* like

a full-fledged etcher. The steam with which then

you stop. And strangle. Thrust the name of this.

(A cramp to open the mouth.)

WHAT THE HEART IS

The heart is a triangle.
With one fewer side, the triangle becomes an opening door.
The door can close into a line.
Is the heart a path when emptied of blood?
The heart is a hallway.
Or panopticon.

As in a tree, from which every other artery travels.
A tree breaks into triangles (leaves) and hearts (leaves).
Sometimes hearts are carved into trees. (By whom?)
But these are not real hearts.

Who are the three balances in the balance?
How does a triangle flatten.
Is it self-sustaining.
Does it take sides.
The heart is rounded, all walls smoothing into a drum.
A drum will sound more or less hollow depending on where you strike it.
So the heart drops its thinning noise.

When the sky is cold, the leaves fall, which makes the tree or heart cold too.
The leaves grow red in the cold.
The scare goes out of them—not the blue.
Which one stands at the triangle's point?
The spear of a heart.
The same doped liquid moving & moving through it.

A heart is a triangle.

A triangle is a heart.

A heart has smoothed sides, with thick tubing coming out.

A triangle is not equal, except when each side is slated.

Will the triangle level to line?

Does the heart <u>become</u> a vein when it is, for that lubbing second, blank?

Of course the heart can close its door.

Like a shut vein, as in when the wrist is pressed down.

After air, an opened vein will close.

Winds close doors.

So what moves through the heart's hallway?

- The heart is a live fist

- The heart is a turnaround

- The heart is a name of a room that is moving

The heart also speaks to a sort of must.

To expansion and puncture the heart sets a life.

When the heart has holes the air can drown it out.

The ground and the sky are against this.

Then the heart lets the song out of its room.

The repeated triangle opens a wall up <u>into</u> . . .

I mean in this light the heart seems very obvious:

    The heart is some kind of frog.

Or in the throat of a frog a balm films over.

The heart in crackles holds no water and not even its own water.

I <u>want</u> the threat of balance, the steer set at center.

In the spinning cable is some truth of story.

The heart's triangle is carried through long clouds.

Draw me out by this water.

DOMESTIC

In the time it takes to set the line, each keyplace
has become vague. In the first, every stone stops
a look. Further christened, the damn door gap holds
a curvature but even we now-met won't revisit that low
clef corner. There there is a horrible face only ended
on the curb. Like paper we cut our gait
from impossible tetrises. Become creatures
that barb the night. Creatures who.

THE *NO REWARD* SESTINAS

Will I use black for your fat boot. The eye uses too.

Come to and I singe eyes in black, the boot of your

mouth—you're mine, too. No boot, but I bruise black, my eye

the eye of your scant black word, too. But I've known boots

and, booted with eyes pinched, I've been your bitch, too. This black

sheens black as boots. You, too, are eyed. If you're the I,

I black your boot—eyes, too.

I do it, that come-to. My me was once far more.

The more I do, our Once (damn that) combs me back to

you. To take more from me, you do it, that trick: *once,*

and *once,* and me in that grey moor. The dew of me

slicks me. So once I'll do it to you—more than that

and that fat me-throe (*more!*)—back. Once, us two were that.

Do that to me once more.

If you can stay, be dumb. I like how the night air

is air still. You are the note. Stay cold like a dumb

song, dumb as air, so like how you have stayed when the

sun's—the crown's—dumbed down. Stay and air what you like:

how like night. The moon (you think *dumb*) is air's last stay.

It stays in like with air. So the day dumbs, and you,

you stay dumb like the air.

I know the way out. My dark room has held more. You'll see—

you are no ship's hold. A way to room with my

face, my hide: you fold rooms back. No damn way this holds.

I hold this, my one way in. You can know the room,

but rooms move. Hold this—no, hold my mouth. You have ways,

the way the room that you once held is my last-known.

No way my room holds you.

For one, my time's not yours. My hand (thumb) did it best—

the best by one. And did, this time, the hand of yours

do your sick best? My hand—my one—is time done. Did

I? Did (not) your own time do best? The one close hand

my hand held—did that one? So you're the best, so time

and time and hands sing best. But did you? You're the one.

One time your hand did best.

When the—my—heart comes a part, would you egg me. Yes.

Say yes to the fat egg. Each heart can, would, spare a

trick, a flat. Yes to *Would you, the soft heart, bloom egg*

to egg? When a—my—heart says yes (soft) the wet wood

bloats. Would an egg know the break? A round yes in heart,

and hearts that would say yes. If eggs are a part hearts,

the heart's a wood egg. Yes.

Tripod Sonnet

The night pulls my beam tight. I stop under-
standing how dazed each day grows outward. Cut
back to noon: did you do me right or cut-
throat? Was I screwed? My scope was under
shutter—a light, I guess, to suffer under.
But I didn't feel a thing against my cut.
You justly didn't shut your mouth to cut
the quiet. I tramped about, whole sky under-
shoe. Meaning you were dumb too.
Please let's close eyes quietly and without
slowing, less my stain, lest I silence to
et cetera. And then just collapse: out
here my skin is all synapse, but without
you I've only my minus to strap to.

3

ELEGY IN WHICH THE FILM DEGRADES

1

She has seen the angle a man shudders into.
The slab of haunch a promise. This woman
whose face opens like a butchers' knot.
"Both my daughters know how to grieve,"
she says, but something beats against
this. Past the window, a blind of rain and dirtier.
If tonight I flatten to a list. "Shabby and hot"
is what she called me, and then I showed her real fire.

2

So this arrow opens its fever: Where there is one
cut there are five. To say nothing of the light
is to say nothing of how a dead room can warp
cankers into lovers. The thickness of sickness
swelters and under its skin. Still the beauty
of the body's swollen crown. All its gilded
mars.   Peel back the spears, the bitter thistle.
        Eat the oily heart.

3

The slab of haunch a promise: a slow answer
takes hold. By hour's end, what is left of her story
will turn clean. What is left
will turn the water at the bed
of the one who breaks into wave.

Tell it like this:
The yarn of the body unravels. Then the body
unravels.

LETTER TO A LAMPSHADE

November in New York has been damp
and long and already the cats have folded
themselves into their own pillowy napes.
We have not spoken, now, for some time.
Outside the window, a patina of frost covers
everything. I drink thick black tea, turn
the oven on for heat, twist my legs into a warm
grey braid. The starlings have left their eggs
to the crows, the crows hum murder
across the sky and across the street
the religious wear the same color, faith's old
dark song. I have stopped speaking to anything
but the body, maybe when he calls me
and tells me to come and kiss him, I wind
my own arm around my own neck
and go out walking. If I were like you, round,
apologetic. If I could seal closed and fall
into a bed wearing only light. It is not even
noon and already someone is dead, the church
thrums and steam comes off my stout red cup
and the cats blink and this is not what I have
to write. Last night he took me to his car
and started driving. I rolled down the window
and blew smoke from the pocket of my mouth
into the pocket of the dark. The moon was a full
white O, wrapped in nothing. We came to a road
so new that under his speed it made a sound
like rain. We were nowhere with a sign. I don't know
how to say this except like this: In the chalky light
was a cow walking slowly down the middle of the road.
November in New York and I am already a small,
primal thing, my body convinced of nothing
but itself. In the field were maybe a dozen more

and as we slowed they slowed and looked at us.
Someone has died. And later, in the dark, when we stopped,
rose out of the car, when he wrapped his coat
around me and the air smelled like fire. The clouds
covered the moon while he kissed my neck. An airplane
flew low over the hills and there was snow on the ground.
A woman walked down the middle of the road, low,
alone. Believe that her face was all I wanted to tell you.

ELEGY IN WHICH I SLEEP RESTFULLY

This is the story that keeps giving: In
   the middle of the winter I become
        unknown to myself. Yes, there's still the hum
of cup after cup: the water boils, gin is poured,
          drunk. I pickle sweetly. My tin heart opens its bag
  of hope, asks for company, beats like a hurricane
of subways. In this city of hard winds, I undress slowly
       before the window, see the shadow
         of smoke from my hot room opening
     against the next building and do not think
anything, go out walking and do not speak to anyone
        about it. The room of this feeling grows
     larger, swells until it can be taken in
        without teeth, like vegetables water-
       warped for hours. I unbolt myself, feed the cat.
    When my lover comes to me I have made myself
          a minor thing. In the evening, I take his lips
   in mine, use that word, *hell*, tell him I will not
            keep. Outside this moment, another room calls
             me, calls for the wall of my chest to fill
      again with air. Elegy in which a slow heart.
       Elegy in which poached song. From the scar
        of this feeling I take another swill.

Flight Sonnet

Arch of anchor or back or long dry
morning. The day is tall and grey
but I am not warming. My grey
mouth opens an arch against the dry
page: blood in the morning, by noon dry
as an archer's back. A long day greys
out like this. I anchor to the page, the grey,
the dumb-warm mouth, and back. Think me dry
or else anchored open, my mouth-long
blood-dumb, my tall page of warming. Back
me back to the noon I arched my longing
against your dumb-long. That morning comes back
like an anchor, that drying the page back:
long live this blood-mouthed, or, greying, live long.

SHINER

Come-to. I give the singe a name: you.
(And you.)

In the light I do not say.

My dress is white and so gone.

Why did I? (Escape to the flood.)

And though mouths are exploded I cannot speak or do not
speak. There is a difference in the letter.

Send it through the cold.
Hold it in the partnered wood.

I betray the case: open the heart and the horse
opens its field and the field is opened by stars too.

Give me a break or break me
against this.

Each chamber of blood.

Quartile.

Behaving.

Air evacuates you, who are dizzy as last rations.

Being and broken: no calm way to circle the thing
that outlasts glass, and its contrivances.

Does gold then burn closer? To bone? To pump
does not sound but still, comes clear:

there's an even clean of rot. You can gel it over,
emboss, though a hole never fills truly.

If every nick syncs, will an orbit of loss grow out from you?
The body is a cavity, too.

Language is hard.
It shines your face.

Mask up. Then, let's make.

Comely bastard.
I'm coming over.
Come here.
I'm coming.

Last appeal to my sense!
The unanswered swarms

(Hurt the bell of me, the round explorer,
explode this stupid)

feel too soon.

Are you awake in the night, or are you night-like really.

When I crown thee thy neck shines like a street.

Understand the path of lasting
from mouth to fast.

It goes drunk slowly on a thick
small fragrance.

Sips air from its own

dipped back.

You tell light by the shapes
it makes in me,

so call me shiner,
the lost and fist-tapped.

I love the strikes of mercury
you love in lieu.

I open my face on every promise.

I do.

Nothing senses towards being
away.

The phrase drops, picks up, sounds rightly
off.

Past argument is a hive
that nightly undrinks itself,

and then. Do I have to behave,
asks the princess.

No one responds Fear.

Or the self-
contained enemy. Or in every question

does skin collapse only its future.

A whole branch of years
trails forward, and like this,

the pill aparts you from the world.

The way I feel is real.

I (in the arch of a pilgrim)
show my pilgrim arch.

And crust to you.

You my lover of the slap-back hero.
You aware of a sickness.

Not in the thing but its shadow.

Can I stay and heel?
Can I have a day?

I will not fasten myself to any botany

but yours.

When the body hurts it draws out

its strangest colors.

When hit does not quit
but gets its good make on.

I brutal the slab you become.

Now I can throw my body like a stone.

Also it's a poultice. It begets the swell
(and begs its own pierce).

Begs

and begs

and begs.

There is, though, no final
climb. You go under-ear

when you greet me. Each blue
links backs, and besides, you

unrest me.
You do not inflate

when my art implodes you.
You are not me,

yet.

Conjugal way
to say this:

your sway opens doors
and does not.

END SONNET

Every wall of me stops asking for you.
You still throw stones, ever the treacher, but
your barb's been worn back. I alone abut
the afternoon, like stitches clipped from you
once falling becomes fell. The slats of you,
too, are tired. They grow inside me but
quietly, approaching the standing butt
end of funny. Forever for months you
were fat as a posey bowl. It's cruel how
I'm saying this, swelling its canker till
my feeling's the joke, stillborn, blunted. How-
ever it's told, love picks up speed until
it cannot pick at all. We plumped this till
it could break anything against its howl.

LAST EVENING: INDEX OF FIRST LINES

The wind on those long avenues and even then I moved alone
Then was last night a department of fear?
There were so many wigs in New York. And corners on fire
This is the only story I know: crack of chin against the toilet
Tongue rank with another beginner angel
What he kissed in me was no meteor or shining pardon
When I rose from my bed I was a watering hole for justice

After it

The Hudson dark   like a rock.
The Hudson   rocking this boat.
There is no   light coming from it.
There is a boat moving blackly
through the night. He holds out
his hand.
    I sit next to a man I never loved but let
    kiss me wetly for two months.
Jersey twinkles in   and out of this.
    When will I turn back
    to a cold,   gold thing? After
the year the river   still presses
with a kiln's glowing shade.
Knots of burnt rubber
unlace   the air.
They were not bodies   because bodies
travel faster.
A whole clock of black   things pitched
into the water.
Fire and a cloudless   coffer, the center
of denatured.
    Here is what I saw.
The ferry is a black yolk,   closed,
thickening   the water.
The gulls   open
their mouths.
    I never loved   any of this:
New York shuttered
like an oven, in the morning,
a wing   of sweat opening
on the sheets.
How it crawls   into bed, stinking
of cinder.   It is slow

and dark   and don't
   I know the creep of straddle
   too. I sit
   at the island's blunt tip
   and watch
the moon ride
the river's deep   black.
    Start here.
The river's deep.   Black
the moon. Ride
   and watch
   at the island's blunt tip,
   too. I sit.
   I know the creep of straddle,
and dark,   the Don't
of cinder. It is slow,
how it crawls   into bed, stinking
on the sheets,
a wing   of sweat opening
like an oven. In the morning,
New York shuttered.
   I never loved   any of this:
their mouths.
The gulls   open,
thickening   the water.
The ferry is a black yolk,   closed.
   Here is what I saw
of denatured:
fire and a cloudless   coffer, the center
of water.
A whole clock of black   things pitched
travel faster.
They were not bodies   because bodies
unlace the air,
knots of burnt rubber
like a kiln's glowing shade.

This year the river   still presses
        to a cold,   gold thing. After,
        when will I turn back?
Jersey twinkles in   and out of this.
        Kiss me wetly for two months.
        I sit next to a man I never loved, but let
his hand.
Through the night, he holds out.
There is a boat moving blackly.
There is no   light coming from it.
The Hudson   rocking this boat.
The Hudson dark   like a rock.

ELEGY IN WHICH I AM NOT WHISKED AWAY

I feel a distance from every corner in the world. I offer
a woman my coat, and she laughs, and she laughs. Is it even
raining? My old eyes bloom against the blue light
of the window. Though every night I am not alone
I am alone during the day, and it disarranges me. It dissects me.
I have stopped looking for the word for it in books, or cigarettes,
or even the huge tongue of moon on my floor. In its mouth
I see only the shadow of last month, how I held the dead
cat in my arms, how much heavier he was dead
than alive, how in the limp light of his body
there was nothing more than the limp light. Maybe this
is how winter always feels, slick and bloated, a sachet
of sweat. I slid my finger down his throat to feel a breath.
Outside, my boots sank into the snow with only that, that
not feeling anything but the sinking. On the empty street,
we made a sound that has no name. And nothing
closed its paw around me that night. It was just heavy.
I wrapped him in my coat and gave the cold flag of him
to someone else. There were no wild crows, blacking out
the sky. There was the gloss of a room, becoming something
darker. That night, I held my weight over the whole mouth
of him, felt his warm slack tongue and did not think,
then, that the body was brutal to be so, to keep crimped
behind its teeth this pocket of heat. There was nothing hot
about what later I gave my body to, how I pulled up my skirt
and the boy said, It's like that, and I said, Yes, and stubbed myself out
against the cold files of his arms. His mouth made these sounds,
and if I was not thirsty then I was dry when he left. This is the answer
to the sweating throat of winter. A scorch of water
for tea. A dead moth floating to the surface. I burn my finger
skimming him out, drop his body into the sink, let the clear wilt of water
take this too.

WHAT MY HEART IS DOING

My heart is lifting   It is leaving my hands and the soles
of my feet   My heart   Like I am not wed
to its dark yolk   Like I am a widow opening
her mouth on a grey slope   And around me
birds are opening their mouths   On a grey
sadness our wings all open   Not wed again
and dark   They are crows   My heart is a lifted
willow bud   Thick and through golden hours
my heart is crashing about itself   Over rivers
my heart lifts air   Over fences my heart lifts
nothing and nothing at midnight is like it
Shadows are weightless so they are not like it
The well on the hill is dry and unlike it   The sky
opens to a swoop and in the dark there are birds
They are crows   They come from everywhere
Their existence is lifting so lifting does not exist
What is is fire and the claw of a dark animal   My heart
is sometimes that animal   Fearless   Lifting its daggers
to the spigot   With its teeth of gold it growls loud
Its widow legs open and dirty soles open   The wings
in the dark become the dark   And there is no dark
Only animal   My heart is lifting that shadow animal

4

Sabbath for a dry season

It was not raining, had only
once rained, would never rain
again. Across the river, the sun
made angels appear stoic.

> In a dark wet room two people
> burn holes in each other. In Styx.
> In the middle of a dope dream
> and the walls are very quiet
> and the sky is burning
>
> and Out There
> in the thin night
> a girl unhooks her bones

*

If Love is

> strings and bark
> the backs of bows hitting rock
> ankles caught at the bottom of a bed
> Jupiter and his 63 moons
>
> If faith is

Dumb Luck.
Sticky lotteries in a pick-up truck.

*

They write books about this sort of magic: It is dark
forever and then it is light. Deer legs buckle into
two shooting stars.

No one is bleeding behind that tree.
No one is writing poems to stop

that make-believe blood.

LAKE SONNET

It was July. It was my birthday. I
was still drinking then. I went with the men
to a lake with no clothing on. The men
who for a year I'd loved hardly and I
walked to the water. All that love hurt my I-
can't-say-what. My hands knew nothing but men
that year. In snow I stand out. Every man
I've ever seen has seen me back. My eyes
sweat from it. Though from there the summer breaks
off, it felt sharp and bright through that last hour,
like glass fired to gold before it breaks
against its own heat. It's soft, and then it breaks,
and, seeing itself, shifts light. For our
trouble, we were cold and wet for an hour.

WHAT MY HEART IS TURNING

My heart. My heart a black flower. Not that. And is my heart an arrow
when in the morning it is crowing. My heart, my heart's crowing,
in the morning there is a blackness to the crowing of my heart. If in the morning
it wakes you. If the sky is black and then it is not black, if the sky travels up
from black and then if my heart is too loud. My heart is awake. If my heart is awake
then my heart is too loud. If in the morning my heart is too loud and it wakes you
and your muffled eyes open and there, there is my heart in the middle of the room.
Or my heart is at the window, crowing and crowing. Then do not touch it
but watch it. So when the sky has traveled its distance
from black and then dark and then not dark and then pink, then,
when my heart has spent its restless quiver. Touch it. Touch my heart so
it burns. Turn and lean forward out of the bed, enter the room and touch my heart
like fire (this black flower, this fever, this pitch, this scrubbed clean, this arch
of morning, this riding night, this black pitch, this fever, this book
in the mouth, this bird in the city, this siphon, this is prisoning, this fever, this pitch,
this mouth on the shelf, this bed on the back, this black city, this arch of bird,
this morning in the mouth, this woman riding night, this pitch
of fire, this bird from the prison, this shelf of fever, this back is not clean,
this arch in the chapter, this book in the morning, this pitch, this fever, this city's
on fire), be fearless, touch me and that turning sun

WEDDING SONG FOR THE LIGHT UNDER THE DOOR

Does a bridle buckle? Does it guide? How does tightness press and does pressing become tightness? Where is the choke here? The keys fall like blunt ghost tongues. The single livelihood of each key.

Do not speak to the lake, or the gather of words you wake sweating with. Sex is what you gave the audience. Each night you bathed in their damp light. Take this heart and soul, and take this might.

The hour you turned five you broke yourself on the arm—you say spoke—of a chair. If I speak it like this—your marriage token broken—what were the salts you later soaked in? Now you open like a scythe.

Silence's sweet hinge is not how this thing swings. Rock your hips against the bed until you feel the shade leaving *that part.*

> The mouth of the untouched as it is being promised (touch). (Touch) the crick of wetness that dots open my clot. It is this (touch) that blooms or is bloomed: and (touch) me all rolled up in ash.

Let's the cradle be and fill up—I mean fill yourselves with your selves. The constellation of shapes spinning all night above two: the place that is too hard for a head.

In this song the spine comes unlaced. In this song the bride goes into the light and her whole life is unmade. This is a song

> When a phrase presses   forth
> Begin the record here: the heart begins too.

Bride is a word that opens out and out and out and returning has changed to a stout silvered thing. It rings. It has clout and a thorn, a tender to its center.

The heart begins two. The sweet castle of you folds up its entrances.

When the bulb of you begins
When the silk-   catching light.

When you plunge.   This plunged.   This hour

a coarse hair rubbing the bone. I am humming to myself as I enter
the room.

WHERE MY HEART IS GOING

When I say that I opened my heart, I mean all of a sudden
the wind stopped moving. The dry sky opened and I was under it,
opening myself, there was no man, there was no woman, I was alone
for the first time in my life and my boots tramped about
and made no noise. I made so no noise that the birds
disappeared. My head spun and I stopped becoming. A white tiger
appeared beside me. I touched the white tiger. I opened my heart.
I rode the white tiger for miles until miles stopped
existing and then we just breathed together. I say we breathed together
and mean purred, we purred like our hearts were made of fire wood.

And there was no light that night, the moon hid itself like a woman
hides herself, and this is familiar, and I will never open my heart
again. I slept for a long time in someone's claws and I will never

Flame of wind. Desert of flaming
sand. Rain of fire. I walked for a long
time to where being blown
about like rain was not a fire, but softly
limning I stopped. Flaming about
like a bad sun. I wound my arm
about his flaming arm. Wind like a bad
wind. I sanded every part of him
down to where being rained on
stopped being liminal. Be rough
with me. Be the soft starch
of flame where I stop blowing
the flame and the flame
is being blown by wind and your sandy
winding arm. I deserted him. And here
we are in the raining.

The birds disappeared. I made noise because I could still
make noise, I opened my mouth and a moon of noise
came out, a soft egg of noise, a cool white globe, I made the noise
I could still make, noise, I made noise, I could still
disappear, I came in a moon of noise, I made still noise.

An owl. A white tiger. A long sloping claw. A moon
made of moon. A man with no name. An owl. A bird
made of bird. A night made of lightlessness. A fire
glowing a deepening coloring. A heart with no heart
inside its heart. A clip on my mouth's roof where his teeth,
where his teeth his teeth were open in my proud egg mouth

And I will never open my mouth again. When I swallowed
his whole chest I swallowed his whole hair. I sloped open, he opened
like a wind of bird, I made the noise that a woman makes when she slopes
open and that was me that night, sloping noise and a whole moon
of noise still inside of me, a noise I bit closed and did not
noise again until my heart had swallowed his whole moon.

I swallowed his whole tiger, I tramped and, tramp under the fire,
I became a slow white claw. Then I gave up boots. I gave up
birds and the deep egg of night. I gave up noise and I became
a deep noise, I opened as a wind opens, and purrs, and swallows
hair and fire and the noise of the burning of the noise, and his teeth
opening in my mouth and I rode that tiger, and together
into the becoming, it was miles before morning, I pretended
to glow and so I glowed.

And this did not exist. A sun opened me away from the fire
and his teeth. No one slowed that night because I was alone
and I was not slowing. His teeth did not exist after they clipped me
in my bird place. The tiger was not a tiger but a low becoming
and in the morning I purred an egg into my own bird heart.

STORY WITH RED HEELS IN ITS MOUTH

She was a princess and I was a princess. This is to say, we were both princesses.
She was the princess of silver before we knew it and also of rubbing. I was the princess
of chainlink and butter and after each recess my girl hands still kissed
with the feeling of clouds where they'd rubbed against granite because yes, even then,
I wanted to save her. Because she was east of where I was I had to travel east
to get to her. Each afternoon I wound my mouth from the mouth of the golden river,
I began to travel and I could feel my teeth turn in. I tuned my path only to the scent
of her perspiration. The sky was sweating also, for it could feel me moving my longing
under it. It was not her, exactly, that I longed for. It was a vacuum rougher than air.
The whole kingdom crept with a static, knowing I was coming. But the birds were
still birds. Our fathers were clouds of the hardest cloud, and I passed under and away
from them. It went on like this, the path was long and if you asked I would say I did not
remember how hard it thrummed against me, how it felt me moving and did not open
like a sea opens, how in fact it closed very hard around my hand and did not open
again until it felt my pulse still live and heavy, and how then the trees fell silent
and the fences fell silent and were golden and silent, and I did not listen to their silence
but kept moving my feet.

Now is a silhouette. Now is a cold ballerina dancing forever. It is after that.
She and I are turning and turning. I rub once more against paper and leave it
tucked behind her throne. And we kick off our red heels. Our red heels go flying
into the white wall and the black wall and the next wall and the next.

NOTES

"Instructions for wooing me (monster that I am)" contains two lines taken from *Roman Holiday*, the 1953 film starring Cary Grant and Audrey Hepburn.

"Dirty Story" paraphrases a lyric from "What Means the World To You," a song by the rapper Cam'ron, off his *S.D.E.* album (2000).

"The *No Reward* Sestinas" are inspired by the life and writings of the Victorian-era diarist and self-described "drudge and slave" Hannah Cullwick. For thirty years, Cullwick was engaged in a proudly sadomasochistic relationship with the British barister Arthur Munby, all the while under his domestic employ. "For I want no reward," she wrote in her journals, after rebuking one of Munby's many unsuccessful marriage proposals.

"Elegy in which I sleep restfully" is inspired by Lillian-Yvonne Bertram.

"Sabbath for a Dry Season" owes a debt to the fifth movement of Hector Berlioz's "Symphonie-Fantastique" (1830).

Fallen from a Chariot, Kevin Prufer
Needlegrass, Dennis Sampson
Laws of My Nature, Margot Schilpp
Sleeping Woman, Herbert Scott
Renovation, Jeffrey Thomson

2004
The Women Who Loved Elvis All Their Lives, Fleda Brown
The Chronic Liar Buys a Canary, Elizabeth Edwards
Freeways and Aqueducts, James Harms
Prague Winter, Richard Katrovas
Trains in Winter, Jay Meek
Tristimania, Mary Ruefle
Venus Examines Her Breast, Maureen Seaton
Various Orbits, Thom Ward

2003
Trouble, Mary Baine Campbell
A Place Made of Starlight, Peter Cooley
Taking Down the Angel, Jeff Friedman
Lives of Water, John Hoppenthaler
Imitation of Life, Allison Joseph
Except for One Obscene Brushstroke, Dzvinia Orlowsky
The Mastery Impulse, Ricardo Pau-Llosa
Casino of the Sun, Jerry Williams

2002
Keeping Time, Suzanne Cleary
Astronaut, Brian Henry
What it Wasn't, Laura Kasischke
Slow Risen Among the Smoke Trees, Elizabeth Kirschner
The Finger Bone, Kevin Prufer
Among the Musk Ox People, Mary Ruefle
The Late World, Arthur Smith

2001

Day Moon, Jon Anderson
The Origin of Green, T. Alan Broughton
Lovers in the Used World, Gillian Conoley
Quarters, James Harms
Mastodon, 80% Complete, Jonathan Johnson
The Deepest Part of the River, Mekeel McBride
Earthly, Michael McFee
Ten Thousand Good Mornings, James Reiss
The World's Last Night, Margot Schilpp
Sex Lives of the Poor and Obscure, David Schloss
Glacier Wine, Maura Stanton
Voyages in English, Dara Wier

2000

Blue Jesus, Jim Daniels
Years Later, Gregory Djanikian
Winter Morning Walks: 100 Postcards to Jim Harrison, Ted Kooser
Mortal Education, Joyce Peseroff
How Things Are, James Richardson
On the Waterbed They Sank to Their Own Levels, Sarah Rosenblatt
Post Meridian, Mary Ruefle
Constant Longing, Dennis Sampson
Hierarchies of Rue, Roger Sauls
Small Boat with Oars of Different Size, Thom Ward